Bridge-building at Norbury.

Staffordshire's Lost Railways

by
David James

Cheddleton Station, 17 April 1954.

Text © David James, 2005.
First published in the United Kingdom, 2005,
by Stenlake Publishing Ltd.,
Telephone: 01290 551122
Printed by Cordfall Ltd., Glasgow, G21 2QA

ISBN 1 84033 346 4

The publishers regret that they cannot supply copies of any pictures featured in this book.

PICTURE ACKNOWLEDGEMENTS

The publishers wish to thank the following for contributing photographs to this book: John Alsop for the front cover, pages 1, 4, 6, 7, 10, 12–19, 22, 30–32, 36, 37, 39–42, 44, 47, 48, the inside back cover and the back cover; and Richard Casserley for pages 2, 5, 8, 9, 11, 20, 21, 23–29, 33, 35, 38, 43, 45 and 46.

INTRODUCTION

By the time George III came to the throne of Britain in 1760, the area around the River Trent's upper basin in North Staffordshire was already on its way to becoming famous as a centre for the pottery industry. This part of England soon became commonly known as the Potteries and included a number of small towns such as Burslem, Hanley, Longton, Newcastle-under-Lyme, Fenton and Tunstall, all of which had china or earthenware factories. However, it was at nearby Stoke that a real centre of excellence for this trade was established under the guidance of men such as Josiah Wedgwood. As the industry expanded, so too did these towns and their resident populations.

To the north-west of the Potteries a substantial coal and ironstone mining industry was also growing and row upon row of blast furnaces soon sprang up to compete with the kilns of the Potteries in polluting Staffordshire's air. The china industry depended heavily upon coal and also on clay brought in from Devon or Cornwall. The latter had to be transported by sea to the port of Liverpool at the mouth of the River Mersey in Lancashire and then transferred overland by horse and cart along poorly maintained trackways. This was a slow and laborious process with only relatively small loads being moved in one go. Clearly the area badly needed new forms of transport

and it was no surprise that Staffordshire was one of the first counties to embrace the canal during the late eighteenth century.

This new era of transportation began in 1777 with the opening of the Trent & Mersey Canal Company's (T&M) 93-mile long waterway which went right through Staffordshire, linking the River Mersey to the navigable section of the Trent at Derwent Mouth between Derby and Nottingham. This triggered off a wave of similar schemes and by the 1830s the canal network in Staffordshire was the dominant means of industrial transport.

However, even though it was a big improvement over the horse and cart the canal was still a slow form of transport and limited in terms of barge size which affected its load-carrying capability. It was not long before its supremacy was being challenged by the railway.

The history of Britain's first working railway, the Stockton & Darlington, is well known as is that of the Liverpool & Manchester Railway (L&M) which opened for business in 1830. Three years later a new company was formed, the Grand Junction Railway (GJR), which aspired to build a line from Newton-le-Willows in Lancashire on the L&M through Warrington into Cheshire via Crewe and down across Staffordshire to Birmingham, the

2

centre of Britain's industrial Black Country. From there trains could continue on to London along other connecting lines then under construction or being promoted, principally the London & Birmingham Railway (L&B).

Somewhat surprisingly, the GJR's line, which opened in 1837, bypassed the Potteries despite the obvious financial benefits of connecting with this booming area. Instead, the GJR built a station at the county town of Stafford and added small halts at Norton Bridge, Whitmore and Madeley to the west of the Potteries for which a horse and coach feeder service was introduced.

As a rival to the GJR, the Manchester & Birmingham Railway (M&B) had been authorised in June 1837 to create a 45½-mile line from Manchester via Stockport and Congleton in Cheshire through the Potteries to link up with the GJR at Chebsey near Norton Bridge in Staffordshire. This route involved building a lengthy tunnel at Harecastle and once construction began the M&B found itself stretched financially.

Meanwhile, the GJR was less than happy about the prospect of sharing its metals with a close competitor and once the L&B opened in 1838 the company was in a strong position through its alliance with the new line to London to block the M&B's plans. When the Manchester & Birmingham's difficulties became common knowledge the GJR approached its struggling rival and suggested that its planned line to Chebsey be abandoned. Instead the M&B was offered a connection at Crewe which would eliminate the GJR's fear of any line built through the Potteries falling into the hands of an opponent with ambitions to build an alternative London–Manchester link.

Despite strong opposition from the Potteries, the M&B accepted the GJR's proposal in order to save itself from financial ruin. Thus by the time 'Railway Mania' gripped Britain in 1845, the Potteries were still without a direct rail connection of their own.

Local leaders all campaigned for railway companies to spread across Staffordshire but without success and eventually these individuals came together to take matters into their own hands. In April 1845 the North Staffordshire Railway (NSR) was incorporated to act as a rival to the GJR.

The new company's original plans included a line from Macclesfield on the M&B in Cheshire past Congleton to Harecastle and then on into the Potteries. It was then to join the GJR at Colwich to the south-east of Stafford. Branch lines were also proposed from Harecastle to Crewe and from Stone to the GJR at Norton Bridge. Also proposed was a brand new line along the Churnet Valley via Leek and Cheadle to Uttoxeter to provide the Potteries with a link to eastern England and, through connections with other lines, a direct route between Manchester (from North Rode on the M&B) and Derby (over track belonging to the newly formed Derby & Crewe Railway).

The GJR was deeply antipathetic towards the NSR, especially after the new company had successfully blocked its plans for a branch line from Basford, near Crewe, down to Stoke. Eventually in late 1845 both companies agreed to make peace. The NSR won the GJR's support for its proposed amalgamation with the Derby & Crewe Railway (D&C) which was planning a line between the two growing railway towns of its title via Stoke and Uttoxeter, with a branch off to Colwich. The D&C also later decided upon two more Staffordshire branches, from Tutbury to Burton-on-Trent and between Stoke and Norton Bridge.

The GJR's agreement to this alliance between the NSR and D&C virtually ruled out any of its own claims to the Potteries. The company passed into history when it became one of the constituents of the newly founded London & North Western Railway (LNWR) during 1846.

By the close of 1848 the NSR had opened lines to Uttoxeter, Burton-on-Trent, South Cheshire and in the Potteries between Stoke and Norton Bridge. The important Churnet Valley line was close to completion and the 'Knotty', as the company was nicknamed after its emblem of a Staffordshire Knot, was well on its way to becoming a dominant force in North Staffordshire. There were others such as the Stafford & Uttoxeter Railway (S&UR), plus one or two privately funded companies as well as intruders from beyond Staffordshire's frontiers like the Great Northern Railway (GNR) – but by and large the 'Knotty' held sway.

Meanwhile, in the south of the county a comparative railway boom was also in progress, prompted by the industrial growth of the neighbouring Black Country. These expanding heavy industries needed south Staffordshire's coal that was being mined around the Cannock district and the railway was seen as the ideal means of exploiting this.

Thus, during 1846, two companies – the South Staffordshire Junction Railway and the Trent Valley, Midlands & Grand Junction Railway – were incorporated by Acts of Parliament to develop lines across the Black Country. Connections to the LNWR were to be provided at Bescot and Lichfield in the Trent Valley. Within months these two companies had united to form the South Staffordshire Railway (SSR) which eventually passed into the ownership of the LNWR.

So the scene was set for many years rivalry across Staffordshire between the NSR and LNWR. This competition continued until the outbreak of the First World War when the railways nationally were taken under temporary Government control for the good of the war effort. The success of this measure was influential in the Grouping Act of 1923 which reduced Britain's multitude of railway companies to just four major operators.

Known collectively as 'The Big Four', these comprised the London, Midland & Scottish (LMS), the London & North Eastern Railway (LNER), the Southern Railway (SR), and the existing Great Western Railway (GWR) which was enlarged to absorb many smaller lines. In Staffordshire the effect of this was that both the NSR and LNWR became part of the LMS network while the LNER also gained a foothold through its absorption of the GNR.

The 1920s and 30s saw the railways decline across much of Staffordshire. Much of this was caused by the exhaustion of many of the county's coal mines. Added to this was a period of industrial unrest as miners sought better working conditions and pay which resulted in strikes that led to a fall in local coal production. Many lines that served such mining areas could not survive the losses in revenue a lack of coal traffic brought. The 1929 Wall Street Crash only added to the economic problems of the time by triggering off a general depression.

Many of the lines affected by the economic downturn could not find salvation in passenger transport as the number of people using such routes had never been particularly high. Even lines that did have a relatively high passenger tally began to suffer as the tram and more especially the motor bus (which was cheaper, more frequent and could go directly to places the railways couldn't) emerged as serious competitors.

This downward trend continued up until the Second World War when once again the railways were brought under government control. The 1939–45 conflict saw Britain's rail system operating at full capacity, moving men, material and munitions around the country en masse while still having to provide a regular (if reduced) passenger and freight service. However, with the investment and funding curtailed to meet war needs the railways suffered deterioration in quality as the war progressed.

When the 'Big Four' regained control after the end of the war they inherited a system that was close to collapse, and with a new Labour government that was committed to nationalising the railway under state control none of them saw any need to lavish funds updating their lines.

Consequently, when British Railways came into being during 1948 it found itself faced with a massive repair bill just to keep the nation's network operating. With money in short supply during the immediate post-war era British Railways had to concentrate upon its more prestigious main-line routes. This left many secondary and branch lines, such as those in Staffordshire, to soldier on in an increasing state of disrepair or neglect.

The growth in car ownership during the 1950s led to a sharp decline in the number of people travelling to and from their places of work each day on the train. The drop was aggravated by an increase in local bus services for those without their own vehicles and against this dual challenge the railways could not compete. As a result passenger trains on many lines across Staffordshire became increasingly unsustainable and were steadily withdrawn.

Another hammer blow came in the shape of a national road-building programme which sparked a boom in lorry-borne freight haulage. This removed at a stroke the local rail network's primary source of income. To add insult to injury, the mighty M6 motorway was built right through the heart of Staffordshire. When it opened in 1961 this monstrous highway was the final nail in the coffin for those lines which had somehow managed to hold on to their goods traffic. The infamous Beeching Report of 1963 merely confirmed the closure of many lines which would have had to shut anyway due to their lack of revenue.

By the 1970s Staffordshire's once considerable railway was but a pale shadow of its former self. The high profile West Coast Main Line (WCML) remained at the heart of what was left, providing high-speed Intercity express services from London to north-west England or Scotland. Elsewhere little remains of what was once a proud and thriving countywide network.

It is these 'lost' lines of Staffordshire that this book illustrates. Readers should be aware that the county is, for the purposes of this book, as defined by the 1974 reorganisation of local government boundaries. As several lines extended beyond Staffordshire's borders I trust that the reader will allow me a certain degree of liberty as to which I have chosen to include. By and large I have attempted to concentrate coverage on those lines which were wholly contained within the county and operated a passenger service.

Finally, please note that all station closure dates given in the text relate to the ending of passenger services only and not necessarily the complete demise of that particular line. Also for the purposes of chronology I have listed the lines in date order of them being opened.

A 2-6-4T locomotive with a passenger train at Wetton Mill.

Tutbury Branch

Horninglow Station, 1951.

	Date
Passenger service withdrawn	11 June 1960
Distance	5½ miles
Company	North Staffordshire Railway

Station closed	*Date*
Horninglow	1 January 1949
Stretton & Clay Mills	1 January 1949
Rolleston-on-Dove	1 January 1949
Tutbury	7 November 1966

Stretton & Clay Mills Station.

Burton-on-Trent, famous for its brewing industry, was on the limits of the NSR's original sphere of influence and it took time for the 'Knotty' to reach it. However, the first step along this road began with the building of a short branch line, originally planned by the Derby & Crewe, from Tutbury on the Uttoxeter–Derby line down and around to the Birmingham & Derby Junction Railway's line into Burton. This small line was hardly one of Burton's more important railways when it opened in September 1848, but for the NSR it was seen as a foothold into new territory. Exactly a year after the branch opened, the 'Knotty' began running freight trains along it into Burton where they transferred on to private sidings which connected up with the powerful Midland Railway.

6   Tutbury Branch

Tutbury Station.

Meanwhile, the original branch had become well known for its use of one, two or three non-corridor coach trains hauled by small tank locomotives. Nicknamed 'Tutbury Jennies' (after the 'Jennie Inn' public house close to Horninglow Station), these services were well liked by local residents. However, operational requirements eventually led to the introduction of 'push-pull' motor trains along the line which improved service timings as they eliminated the need for a locomotive change-of-ends at Tutbury or Burton-on-Trent. Despite this the occasional tank engine and carriages still put in an appearance. Like so many others, the branch suffered from increased road and tram competition after the First World War. This competition was so strong that in 1949 the newly formed British Railways had to close all three intermediate stations along the line due to falling passenger numbers. The last passenger trains ran in June 1960 and the line, which had never attracted any major freight services despite its connections to Burton, was closed completely.

Walsall to Wichnor Junction

		Date
Passenger service withdrawn	18 January 1965	
Distance	17¼ miles	
Company	South Staffordshire Railway	

Stations closed	Date
Rushall	18 January 1965
Pelsall	18 January 1965
Brownhills	18 January 1965
Hammerwich	18 January 1965

Stations closed	Date
Lichfield City *	18 January 1965
Lichfield Trent Valley Junction **	18 January 1965
Alrewas	18 January 1965

* First station closed in 1871; replaced with a new one a little to the west of the original location.

** First Trent Valley Junction station closed in 1871; replaced by a new facility a quarter mile to the south.

Pelsall Station, 12 May 1956.

Brownhills Station.

Despite its title, the South Staffordshire Railway (SSR) concentrated most of its initial efforts building lines across the Black Country around Wolverhampton, Walsall and Birmingham. The company had been formed in 1846 and at first received the backing of both the Midland Railway and the LNWR who feared the advance of the broad-gauge GWR into the West Midlands. Based at Walsall, the SSR soon became arguably the most important railway company within the Black Country and decided to extend its influence northwards into the lucrative coal mining districts of Staffordshire around Cannock. This began with the building of a new line from Walsall to Wichnor Junction in Staffordshire, close to Burton-on-Trent where the Midland had several lines. This branch was to be the artery from which the SSR spread out across south Staffordshire. The line opened in April 1849 with several intermediate stops. Another station, Trent Valley, was added a year later where the branch crossed the main line between Rugeley and Tamworth. The SSR intended that its new route should primarily be for goods traffic but a passenger service began from June 1849. An agreement was reached with the Midland for a timetable of four trains each way every day between Walsall and Burton to connect with that company's services and it was not long before the branch took on a distinctly Midland flavour.

Alrewas Station.

However, in 1850 the SSR's board split over a proposal that the branch be leased out privately. Both the LNWR and Midland's supporters objected to the idea and it was initially defeated. Then, though, both companies reneged on their guarantees to honour dividends to the SSR's shareholders so the plan was revived and this time accepted. With Parliamentary approval for the scheme secured, the SSR agreed in 1851 to lease the Walsall–Wichnor Junction line out to an engineer of Irish descent named John Robinson McClean. Unusually the agreement was for a lengthy period of 21 years. However, after a decade of running the line McClean cancelled his contract due to disagreements with the SSR board. The branch, along with all 29 of the SSR's locomotives, was then transferred to the LNWR. This move upset the Midland, which hated the idea of the LNWR being able to strengthen its power around Burton-on-Trent by running services into the town over Midland metals. The familiar pattern of declining passenger numbers after the Second World War, increased car ownership and stiff competition from the growing road network all conspired to push the branch into decline. As a result passenger services were withdrawn by British Railways in January 1965 with freight continuing until 1984 before the route was finally closed. Today, however, a section of the branch has been reopened between Lichfield and Lichfield Trent Valley (a new station). Responding to local commuter needs British Rail (BR) restored this section for services to Birmingham New Street in October 1989.

The Churnet Valley Line

Passenger service withdrawn	4 January 1965
Distance	30 miles
Company	North Staffordshire Railway

Stations closed	Date
North Rode	7 May 1962
Bosley	7 November 1960
Rushton	7 November 1960
Cliffe Park *	7 November 1960
Rudyard Lake **	7 November 1960
Leek	4 January 1965
Leek Brook ***	31 October 1959
Cheddleton	4 January 1965

Stations closed	Date
Consall	4 January 1965
Kingsley & Froghall ****	4 January 1965
Oakamoor	4 January 1965
Alton	4 January 1965
Denstone Crossing Halt	4 January 1965
Rocester	4 January 1965
Uttoxeter (Dove Bank)	1 October 1881

* Originally named Rudyard Lake from 1905–25 and reclassified as a halt during 1940.
** Originally named Rudyard for Horton until 1925.
*** Existed as an exchange platform on down side only.
**** Originally named Froghall until May 1907.

North Rode Station,
29 April 1933.

Bosley Station.

The Churnet Valley line, opened by the NSR in July 1849, was one of the original lines proposed during that company's formation and was intended to provide a connection from Manchester via North Rode in Cheshire to Uttoxeter and beyond. One of its principal aims later on was to capture the lucrative stone transportation business around Caldon Low from the existing canal system. Where the branch commenced at North Rode there was a thriving dairy farming community and immediately south of the station there the line curved away into the Churnet Valley. The stop at Cliffe Park, originally known as Rudyard Lake, was close to a reservoir created to serve the nearby canals. It was here that an architect from Stoke named Kipling proposed to his fiancé. Later, they had a son – Rudyard.

The major station along the line was built at Leek as this town was not only the largest within the Churnet Valley but also had a well-established silk industry and local market. Both these brought in valuable business for the railway as did the town's monthly horse sales. Nearby was Leek Brook which later became an important junction with two connections provided. The southern one, created in 1867, gave a link to the Stoke–Bradnop, Waterhouses and Hulme End line. The northern one, established in 1905, gave access to the Leek & Manifold Valley Railway, a light narrow gauge system. The two junctions were connected via a triangular track layout and between them there was a series of sidings for the collection and distribution of stone traffic from Caldon Quarry. Industrial goods trains also gathered here from factories further down the Churnet for onward dispatch to Stoke and the main line. The copper industry had set up a base in the Churnet Valley as early as 1734 when a mill was opened at Alton by one Thomas Patten who had already built similar works at Warrington in Lancashire. The Alton site closed down in 1829 as the Patten family moved down river to Oakamoor before eventually selling out to Thomas Bolton and his sons.

Leek Station.

Kingsley & Froghall Station.

Serving Bolton's factory, which was expanding rapidly due to the invention in the 1850s of the telegraph (which relied heavily upon copper wiring), became a key purpose of the line and new sidings were added not just at Oakamoor but also later at Froghall where the Bolton family established a second works in 1890. Froghall also doubled as the original rail point for limestone from Caldon which arrived via a horse-drawn tramway. The branch also served the local aristocracy for close to Alton the Earl of Shrewsbury had a lavish mansion named Alton Towers. To please the Earl the NSR built its adjoining station in the same architectural fashion to that of his home and added a unique series of luggage lifts to convey his baggage or goods directly from the station up to his estate.

Oakamoor Station.

In Uttoxeter, famous for its racecourse, a brand new station was constructed at Dove Bank which incorporated an exchange platform with the neighbouring Bridge Street Station on the line to Stoke. This arrangement lasted until 1881 when a new line was laid from Uttoxeter North to Bridge Street where new facilities were added to handle trains working the Churnet Valley, thereby enabling Dove Bank to be closed. The Churnet branch thrived for many years with a daily timetable of five trains in each direction running at three-hourly intervals for many years. Through services to Manchester and Derby (via Uttoxeter) also used the route on a regular basis while freight trains abounded, especially during the hours of darkness. The line could have achieved even more as it potentially offered the shortest route for Manchester to London trains but most of these continued to be routed via Stoke or Crewe despite the extra journey times involved.

Alton Station.

Even the creation of the direct Stoke–Leek link had little impact upon the branch which, after the 1923 Grouping Act, became the property of the LMS. In that same year the current Earl of Shrewsbury disposed of his Alton estate to a development consortium which turned it into a well-known amusement park. By the 1930s, though, the effects of the Great Depression were beginning to be felt along the line as was the stiffening competition from trams running across several towns in the valley. The emergence of the motor bus provided even more of a threat and passenger numbers began to fall. Revenue and services briefly revived during the Second World War, only to go back into a slow decline in the wake of the railways being nationalised during 1948. In an effort to reduce operating costs and increase profits from the line British Railways closed the northern end of the branch between North Rode and Leek to passenger traffic in 1960. This was then followed by the withdrawal of such services between Leek and Uttoxeter in January 1965.

Rocester Station.

Freight traffic carried on even though much of the line had by this point in time been singled. Workers' trains also continued to ferry in employees of Thomas Bolton & Sons and also those of the British Industrial Sand (BIS) works at Oakamoor. Even here there was some reduction in terms of numbers for Bolton's closed its Oakamoor site to save money during 1963, concentrating copper production at Froghall instead. Goods trains carried on running in ever-diminishing numbers from Stoke to Oakamoor and Froghall via Leek Brook until the middle of 1970. Today, the branch is little more than a lengthy siding with approximately eight miles of track still in situ (all of it singled) for the occasional freight turn.

Rocester to Ashbourne

		Date
Passenger service withdrawn	1 November 1954	
Distance	7 miles	*Stations closed*
Company	North Staffordshire Railway	Norbury & Ellaston 1 November 1954
		Clifton 1 November 1954
		Ashbourne 1 November 1954

Norbury & Ellaston Station, c.1910.

This branch opened in 1852 as a cross-county line from Rocester in the Churnet Valley to Ashbourne in Derbyshire. At first its traffic was poor but matters improved significantly once the rival LNWR's line from Buxton in Derbyshire (famous as a spa town) arrived at Ashbourne in 1899. This provided an alternative through route from Manchester via the Peak District on to the NSR's system and thence down to Birmingham or beyond. This journey measured 194 miles, whereas the traditional Manchester–Birmingham route over the former GJR line via Crewe was ten and a half miles shorter so it never really caught on as a viable option. After the LNWR arrived at Ashbourne, the North Staffordshire improved its line between there and Rocester. Despite this the route was still not considered suitable for express trains and so remained very much a local line. The NSR's original station at Ashbourne later became a goods depot when an altogether lesser structure was opened to serve both its needs and those of the LNWR.

Ashbourne Station, c.1910.

At its peak the Rocester–Ashbourne branch operated four trains in each direction every week day, with two of these featuring through carriages for onward transfer to Buxton or Birmingham. As passenger figures declined after the Second World War British Railways began employing pairs of non-corridor coaches along the route, hauled by ex-LMS 2-6-4 tank locomotives, to work most services. Gradually the whole line's purpose came into question despite many local inhabitants launching an appeal to keep it open. British Railways was unimpressed and the entire branch closed to passenger trains in November 1954. The track work remained in situ and was used by freights plus the occasional winter relief train for the Peak District until the middle of 1964.

Locomotive No. 2264, heading coach No. 25825 with the 5.53 p.m. service from Buxton to Uttoxeter, at Ashbourne on 3 May 1934.

Cannock to Rugeley

Passenger service withdrawn	18 January 1965
Distance	7.9 miles
Company	Cannock Mineral Railway

	Date
Stations closed	
Hednesford (CMR)	18 January 1965
Brindley Heath	18 January 1965

Cannock was reached by a railway from Walsall in the Black Country during the early part of 1858. However, this was the end of the line, for between Cannock and the town of Rugeley over in the Trent Valley lay an area of rough hilly terrain known as the Chase. This could only be crossed by poorly maintained pathways and a railway would have made such a journey much easier and quicker if it had been provided. Nobody at the time though saw any need to do so, especially as constructing such a line would have been a demanding and expensive engineering task. That all changed with the opening up of coal seams around Hednesford, just outside of Cannock. Having already built the Walsall–Cannock line, the LNWR was persuaded of the benefits of extending this line as far as Rugeley (which the company's main line down the Trent Valley already passed through) and so helped create the Cannock Mineral Railway or CMR to provide just such a link. The extension finally opened in November 1859 and was worked on behalf of the CMR by LNWR locomotives. Ten years later, despite the efforts of the NSR to secure the line for itself, the LNWR fully absorbed the CMR. The branch provided numerous sidings with tiny halts to various pits and these were used to carry coal to Hednesford where it was marshalled for onward transit to Rugeley or Walsall. The CMR also provided trains that took local miners to or from the coalface in carriages fitted with bare wooden seats. This spartan accommodation was thought necessary because most of the mines did not have washing facilities so the men had to travel home after a long shift underground caked in coal dust and grime and the LNWR didn't want its passenger coaches being spoiled! In time these miners' services became known as 'Paddy Trains' (because many of the mine workers were Irish immigrant labourers). As the coal industry declined during the 1920s so too did the line's fortunes. Passenger numbers fell as the bus came along and many mineworkers took to using this new form of public transport as it was not only cheaper but also took them right to the pit entrance unlike the railway line. As a result the 'Paddy Train' came to an end during this period. The line soldiered on until all passenger traffic was completely withdrawn in January 1965. Freight operations survived however and in 1989 the line as far as Hednesford was reopened by British Rail for passenger trains serving the local commuter market.

The Biddulph Branch

	Date
Passenger service withdrawn	11 July 1927
Distance	14.6 miles
Company	North Staffordshire Railway

Stations closed	Date
Carter's Crossing	before 1901
Fenton Manor	6 May 1956
Bucknall & Northwood	7 May 1956
Ford Green *	11 July 1927
Chell Halt	11 July 1927

Stations closed	Date
Black Bull **	11 July 1927
Knypersley Halt	11 July 1927
Biddulph ***	11 July 1927
Mossley Halt	13 April 1925

* Originally named Ford Green, then renamed Ford Green & Smallthorne.
** Originally named Black Bull (Childplay), then renamed Brindley Ford.
*** Originally known as Gillow Heath.

Fenton Manor Station, 4 September 1954.

Black Bull Station, 1952.

This line received Parliament's consent in July 1854 as a route along the Biddulph Valley, from Stoke to Congleton in Cheshire, for coal services. Indeed, freight trains began running as soon as the line opened in 1864 and it was a few months before the first passenger service was provided by the NSR in order to satisfy local demands. However it was coal, the black gold of Staffordshire, that was king along the line. Pits surrounded it at places such as Whitfield, Northwood and Birchenwood, and these ensured that it soon made a healthy profit. As such, when the LMS took charge during the early 1920s the branch was among one of the first after Grouping to lose its regular passenger service. The LMS believed that the numbers being carried were not high enough to warrant continuing with, especially as coal trains brought in more revenue, so in July 1927 the last one was run. This left the branch working as a freight-only line and such traffic remained heavy despite the decline of Staffordshire's coal industry over the interwar period. The LMS opposed the running of privately owned goods trains along the line (whereas the NSR had tolerated them) and so these too were stopped during 1931. The line survived into the British Railways era but at the end of 1963 it ceased to be a through route after its spur to the main line at Congleton was cut in preparation for the electrification of the West Coast Main Line in that area. Five years after this the entire line north of Biddulph was shut down. However, coal trains continued traversing what remained of the line into the 1970s, even while the mining sector continued shrinking. Trains called as far as Victoria Colliery near Biddulph until December 1975 when mining at that pit came to an end. The neighbouring Whitfield mine closed the following July, succeeded by the link to the pit at Ford Green eleven months later. The final complete mile of trackwork between Ford Green and Milton Junction, a sad reminder of the branch's former glory, was finally taken out of use in March 1979. This act left just a few hundred yards open to enable goods traffic travelling from Stoke via Bucknall and Milton Junction (see the next section for details) to pass over on to the remnants of the Churnet Valley branch at Leek Brook.

Bucknall & Milton Junction to Leek Brook

	Date		Stations closed	Date
Passenger service withdrawn	7 May 1956		Stockton Brook	7 May 1956
Distance	6 miles		Endon	7 May 1956
Company	North Staffordshire Railway		Wall Grange	7 May 1956
			* Originally known as Bucknall.	
Stations closed	Date			
Bucknall & Northwood *	7 May 1956			
Milton	7 May 1956			

Milton Station, 4 September 1954.

Stockton Brook, 4 September 1954.

Authority for this branch, from the main line south of Stoke via Bucknall on the Biddulph Valley line, to connect with the Churnet Valley at Leek Brook was given by Parliament in July 1863. It was intended to provide additional direct access to the industrial areas of Oakamoor and the quarries at Caldon Low. However constructing the new line took over four years due to a shortage of money and some difficult engineering requirements that involved the use of extensive earthworks.

Wall Grange, 11 April 1955.

When the branch finally opened for business in November 1867 it was immediately cleared for both passenger and goods traffic. Although built as a single line the branch was never doubled despite relatively heavy use during its earlier years. Decline set in during the 1920s and 30s and continued through into the British Railways' era. The decision was taken to withdraw the loss-making passenger services and this was done in 1956, although goods traffic carried on into the following decade when the branch also found favour as a secondary route for football specials. Today, the trackbed remains in use as a freight access route to the Churnet Valley but services are somewhat infrequent.

Stafford to Uttoxeter

Passenger service withdrawn	4 December 1939	Date
Distance	13 miles	
Company	Stafford & Uttoxeter Railway	

Stations closed		Date
Stafford Common *		4 December 1939
Stafford Common (Air Ministry)		30 November 1976
Salt & Sandon **		4 December 1939

Stations closed		Date
Ingestre & Weston		4 December 1939
Chartley ***		4 December 1939
Grindley		4 December 1939

* Originally known as The Common when first opened in 1874.

** Known as Salt until 1904.

*** Named Stowe until 1874.

Stafford Common, 23 March 1957.

The Stafford & Uttoxeter Railway (S&UR) was authorised by Parliament in July 1862 to build a connection across Staffordshire from the LNWR-owned Crewe–Wolverhampton line and the NSR's Stoke–Derby line. Building this link was to prove surprisingly difficult due to the requirement for a 321-yard long tunnel at Bromshall and a deep cutting near Hopton that required blasting through solid rock. Despite these vicissitudes, the line opened in December 1867 and the S&UR was granted running rights at either end over the LNWR's tracks into Stafford Station and the NSR's Uttoxeter Bridge Street Station. Both these locations offered the prospect of connections with other trains running on different lines. The line soon began catering for the growing population to the north of Stafford, along with race-goers from all over the country who flocked to the course at Uttoxeter. Despite this revenue the S&UR was in dire financial trouble by 1879 as a result of hostility from both the LNWR and the NSR, both of which opposed the S&UR's growing closeness to the GNR. Both also coveted the Stafford–Uttoxeter link for themselves.

Salt & Sandon, 23 March 1957.

In response, the S&UR sought support from the GNR and won Parliamentary approval for the latter to run trains along its metals. At the same time a settlement was reached with the NSR that enabled the S&UR and the GNR to continue using that company's stretch of track between Bromshall Junction (at the end of Stafford & Uttoxeter territory) and Bridge Street Station. In return the NSR was permitted to run its trains over the S&UR, much to the LNWR's fury. Originally, when it had backed the S&UR, the GNR had harboured ambitions to extend its services through into neighbouring Shropshire and then on to Central Wales. This would have provided a powerful cross-country route but it never came to pass for the LNWR, which had the most to lose if the extension had gone ahead, managed to get the scheme rejected in Parliament. Following the agreement between the GNR and NSR, the Stafford–Uttoxeter link saw an increase in traffic but increasingly the S&UR found itself being subjected to the GNR's will. This dominance crystallised in 1881 when the GNR purchased the company outright. Once in complete control the GNR introduced new services such as a Stafford to Derby express and began providing excursions across to Eastern England's coastal resorts. Freight traffic also began to intensify following the establishment of a salt industry at Stafford Common during 1877. Transporting milk also became lucrative business and milk-processing plants were soon up and running at Ingestre and Uttoxeter to supply not just local needs but also much of London too. Moved in purpose-built tankers or large churns, this service lasted up until the 1930s when road transport took over.

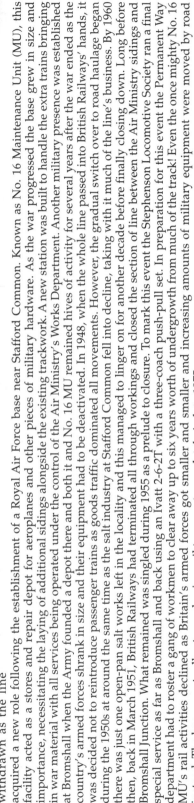

Grindley, 23 March 1957.

During 1923 the GNR became a component of the new LNER even though geographically speaking it would have made more sense for the Stafford–Uttoxeter line to become part of the LMS. As it was, the line remained popular under its new ownership throughout the 1920s and 30s. Race-goers also continued to use it for specials. At the start of the Second World War passenger services along the line were cut back sharply to just one train in each direction per day as rail resources were switched to areas that benefited the war effort. Then, in December 1939, all regular passenger turns were completely withdrawn as the line

acquired a new role following the establishment of a Royal Air Force base near Stafford Common. Known as No. 16 Maintenance Unit (MU), this facility acted as a stores and repair depot for aeroplanes and other pieces of military hardware. As the war progressed the base grew in size and importance, necessitating the laying of additional sidings alongside the existing trackwork. A new station was built to handle the extra trains bringing in war material with all services being operated under the control of the Air Ministry's Works Department. Another military presence was established at Bromshall when the Army founded a depot there and both it and No. 16 MU remained hives of activity for several years after the war ended as the country's armed forces shrank in size and their equipment had to be deactivated. In 1948, when the whole line passed into British Railways' hands, it was decided not to reintroduce passenger trains as goods traffic dominated all movements. However, the gradual switch over to road haulage began during the 1950s at around the same time as the salt industry at Stafford Common fell into decline, taking with it much of the line's business. By 1960 there was just one open-pan salt works left in the locality and this managed to linger on for another decade before finally closing down. Long before then, back in March 1951, British Railways had terminated all through workings and closed the section of line between the Air Ministry sidings and Bromshall Junction. What remained was singled during 1955 as a prelude to closure. To mark this event the Stephenson Locomotive Society ran a final special service as far as Bromshall and back using an Ivatt 2-6-2T with a three-coach push-pull set. In preparation for this event the Permanent Way department had to roster a gang of workmen to clear away up to six years worth of undergrowth from much of the track! Even the once mighty No. 16 MU's rail activities declined as Britain's armed forces got smaller and smaller and increasing amounts of military equipment were moved by road instead. The base eventually stopped using rail transport completely in late 1975.

Stoke to Market Drayton

Passenger service withdrawn	2 March 1964
Distance	16.2 miles
Company	North Staffordshire Railway

Stations closed	*Date*
Hartshill & Basford Halt	20 September 1926
Newcastle-under-Lyme	2 March 1964
Brampton Halt	2 April 1923
Liverpool Road Halt	29 February 1964
Knutton Halt	20 September 1926
Crown Street Halt	7 June 1949
Silverdale	7 May 1956
Keele *	7 May 1956
Keele Park	5 March 1907
Madeley Road **	20 July 1931
Pipe Gate (for Woore)	7 May 1956
Norton-in-Hales	7 May 1956
Market Drayton	7 May 1956

* Originally named Keele for Madeley.
** Originally known as Madeley Manor.

During the eighteenth century a lucrative mining industry was created around the village of Silverdale and to exploit this the NSR opened a freight-only line from its base at Stoke to Silverdale via Newcastle-under-Lyme during 1852. The final stretch of this line utilised the privately owned Silverdale & Newcastle Railway, which had been built in 1850 without powers by a local ironworker named Ralph Sneyd. Sneyd's line served his works and gave him a direct link onto the NSR's tracks to Stoke. Such was the power and influence of the county's industrialists, such as Sneyd, that they could virtually command a railway to come to them rather than the other way around and if the railway company was reluctant to do so then they would just go ahead and build lines of their own. After opening up the route the NSR balked at the idea of expanding it any further westwards towards the county border with Shropshire. However, the LNWR soon began to stir up trouble by supporting a proposal from the Shrewsbury & Potteries Junction Railway (S&PJ) to build a link to Silverdale off its planned line from Wellington to Crewe.

Silverdale Station, 28 August 1954.

Madeley Road Station, 18 October 1952.

The NSR managed to get this idea blocked but then the expanding broad-gauge GWR came on to the scene with the notion of a line across North Shropshire via Market Drayton and on up to Manchester during 1862. The idea of an 'outsider' pushing through their traditional domains united the NSR and LNWR in opposition to the scheme. However, the GWR was no minnow that could be easily deterred and so to finally prevent the plan from becoming a reality the 'Knotty' was forced to expand into Shropshire itself from the vicinity of Silverdale. To do so, the existing Silverdale & Newcastle had to become a public body, which it did in 1859, and the following year it was leased to the NSR. As part of the expansion programme a passenger service was introduced in 1862 and two years later Parliament gave its approval for the line to be carried forward as far as Market Drayton.

Pipe Gate Station, c.1910.

This was eventually completed and opened in February 1870. The building work had also included a short spur off to the LNWR station at Madeley and in a rare act of co-operation the 'Knotty' granted its chief rival full running rights over the newly completed link. Early on in its life the branch was busy. Timber, cattle and diary products were generated around Pipe Gate, bringing in much valuable income for the line as did the nearby racecourse of the same name which opened in 1885. Another course was created at Keele Park by the Sneyd family, but this only lasted until 1901. Elsewhere, the mining industry generated vast amounts of traffic – so much so in fact that the local pit owners came to an arrangement with the NSR to run private passenger trains between Newcastle-under-Lyme and their coalfields in order to transport the miners to or from the pits using numerous tiny halts.

Market Drayton Station, c.1911.

By the early part of the twentieth century though, the NSR was forced to introduce railcars along the line in an effort to cut costs as passenger numbers dropped due to a local recession and the arrival of local tram services. The LMS took charge in the 1920s and laid on additional trains in an effort to win back passengers, but without much success. Somehow the branch clung on to life and it was not until 1956 that British Railways was forced to scrap passenger trains along part of its length between Silverdale and Market Drayton. Services between Stoke and Silverdale carried on for another eight years before they too were withdrawn; freight survived until 1966. Today, only a short section of the line remains in use for coal traffic around Silverdale. This can only be accessed via a spur from the West Coast Main Line between Stafford and Crewe known as the Madeley Chord.

The Loop

	Date
Passenger service withdrawn	2 March 1964
Distance	7¾ miles
Company	North Staffordshire Railway

Stations closed	Date
Kidsgrove Liverpool Road *	2 March 1964
Market Street Halt	2 March 1964
Newchapel & Golden Hill	2 March 1964
Pitts Hill	2 March 1964

Stations closed	Date
Tunstall Junction	17 February 1964
Burslem	2 March 1964
Cobridge	2 March 1964
Waterloo Road	4 October 1943
Hanley	2 March 1964

* Originally named Kidsgrove; renamed in 1944.

Cobridge Station, 1952.

This branch was intended to serve six closely packed towns of the Potteries, thereby avoiding the heavily congested main line route. However, despite strong local appeals, it was not until 1865 that the NSR applied for and was granted permission to go ahead. No sooner had this approval been signed then a national economic slump occurred, forcing the 'Knotty' to consider abandoning the entire project. But local feeling in support of the line was high and the NSR's suggestion to Parliament was defeated after heavy lobbying. So the company next came up with the idea of using a narrow gauge system, but that too was rejected. Thus, construction began at Burslem in July 1870 and five years later the branch finally opened for freight traffic and provided a useful through link from Etruria via Burslem and Tunstall up to Kidsgrove. A passenger service also began in late 1875. Despite its earlier misgivings the NSR took to encouraging locals to use the line by adding another stop near Kidsgrove called Market Street Halt in 1909. There was only one obvious disadvantage to the line and that was where it joined the main line near Harecastle (because of the location trains had to set back from the branch onto the main line and into the station, which took time and delayed other services). In 1923 the line passed into LMS ownership. By that time the Loop had already begun to feel the effects of increased competition from trams and buses. Despite this, an average of 20 trains per day used the line up until the outbreak of the Second World War. Harecastle Station was renamed Kidsgrove Central in October 1944, forcing the Loop's Kidsgrove stop to become Kidsgrove Liverpool Road in order to avoid confusion. The demise of Staffordshire's coal industry saw a sharp drop in the volume of freight using The Loop in the postwar era. Passenger figures also continued to decline in the face of improved bus connections and the onset of mass car ownership. As revenue from the branch tumbled so British Railways was forced to implement cost-cutting measures in the form of fewer trains. This only had limited success and in March 1964 all passenger services were completely withdrawn. Freight traffic rolled on until 1967 when the Loop was finally closed and track lifting began. However, in June 1971 a partial section was reopened between Kidsgrove and Goldenhill to enable trains to serve the opencast mine at Park Farm. Lengthy Merry-Go-Round services appeared and continued to use this short stretch until January 1976. Today, much of where the branch once stood is now a public pathway known as the Loop Greenway.

The Pinnox Branch

Passenger service withdrawn	17 February 1964
Distance	1.36 miles
Company	North Staffordshire Railway

Stations closed	*Date*
Tunstall Junction	17 February 1964

Officially this short line, which opened for goods trains in 1875, was called the Tunstall Lower Branch and was built to provide a link from the main line at Longport to the Loop at Tunstall Junction. Locally, however, it was popularly referred to as the Pinnox Branch after the exchange sidings which were built along the line for the mines of the Chatterley–Whifield area. From these sidings private spurs run by mining companies carried on eastwards into the Biddulph Valley. The Pinnox was heavily used by freight trains, mostly coal, throughout its life, but a passenger service was introduced in July 1892. This never really caught on, but managed against all the odds to survive until February 1964 before being withdrawn. At the same time new access routes were opened to the nearby pits from the Biddulph Valley. This enabled British Railways to re-route most of its freight services away from the branch and this led to its closure.

The Audley Branches

Passenger service withdrawn	27 April 1931
Distance	7 miles
Company	North Staffordshire Railway

Stations closed	*Date*
Leycett	27 April 1931
Halmerend	27 April 1931
Audley *	27 April 1931
Alsager Road **	27 April 1931

* Also known as Audley & Bignall End.
** Originally named Talke & Alsager Road; renamed in 1902.

Running off the Stoke–Market Drayton line near Keele a branch to Harecastle via Audley was approved in July 1864. In fact the line was more of a collection of smaller routes serving the local coal pits at Audley, Bignall Hill, Rookery and Jamage. The NSR found constructing this branch to be surprisingly difficult and time consuming, with flooding and subsidence being the two most common hindrances. In addition many of the short spurs to the pits were of substandard construction. This meant that the line as a whole could only be used for freight trains at first and it was not until the summer of 1880, after the 'Knotty' had refurbished the existing trackwork and signalling to an acceptable standard, that a passenger service could be implemented. In the wake of the First World War many of the mines surrounding the line closed down as they had been all but exhausted and were no longer economically viable. Consequently, thousands of miners lost their livelihoods and many were forced to move away from the area in search of work. This had a knock-on effect on the branch with both freight and passenger traffic declining sharply. In 1931 the LMS took the decision to withdraw all passenger trains due to a lack of demand. Freight carried on for another thirty years but this too declined as more and more pits closed. For example, the spurs to the Jamage and Bignall Hill mines shut in 1947 and 1963 respectively. In the final years of its existence, before it was finally closed for good, the line rarely saw a goods train pass beyond Audley.

The Cheadle Branch

Passenger service withdrawn	17 June 1963
Distance	4 miles
Company	Cheadle Railway Mineral & Land Limited

Stations closed		*Date*
Cheadle		17 June 1963
Tean *		1 June 1953
Cresswell		7 November 1966

* Originally known as Totmonslow; renamed in 1906.

Cheadle Station, c.1905.

A line to Cheadle (east of Stoke) was considered in the early 1850s after local residents complained that their needs had been overlooked when the Stoke–Uttoxeter main line and Churnet Valley branch had been built. Various schemes were suggested, but it was not until August 1888 that Parliament approved a branch from Cresswell (on the Stoke–Uttoxeter line) to Cheadle. This was the idea of the Cheadle Railway Mineral & Land Limited, a private company backed by the NSR. No sooner had work on the new line begun than a series of problems was encountered.

A 2-4-0T locomotive at Tean Station.

Firstly, the CRM&LL was so short of money that construction had to be halted while the company attempted to resolve its financial difficulties. Then a major tunnel had to be engineered below a 700-feet high ridge. Measuring 977 yards in length, this tunnel had to be approached from a steep gradient that at times reached 1 in 40 and although it was a great achievement the tunnel was to prove a maintenance nightmare that constantly drained the CRM&LL's limited finances. The line finally opened for business in January 1901. Upon arriving at Cresswell, services could carry on up the main line to Stoke and connect with the Loop. Goods traffic was lighter than had been anticipated and largely revolved around the output of the two local pits at Draycott and New Haden. Both of these closed in 1906 and the loss of revenue forced the CRM&LL into liquidation. As a result the NSR stepped in during 1907 and increased services along the branch as well as reopening the New Haden mine. However, subsidence caused by mining affected the branch's notorious tunnel. This was dramatically illustrated in November 1918 when part of the tunnel's roof caved in at the Cheadle end and completely blocked the track for several weeks until repairs could be made.

Totmonslow Station (later renamed Tean), 1 January 1907.

Continuing problems with the tunnel dogged the line even after the company got Parliament to approve the building of a diversionary link in 1931 to avoid the high ground which had necessitated the tunnel's construction in the first place. This new stretch opened in November 1933 and was one of the few pieces of rail building undertaken by the LMS in Staffordshire between the wars. Despite this improvement traffic along the line declined steadily as it was cheaper and more convenient to travel between Cheadle and Cresswell by bus than train. In 1943 the exhausted New Haden pit was closed again, although the loss in freight revenue this caused was partially offset by the opening of a small brick factory near the site of the old mine. In 1953 Tean Station was closed by British Railways due to a lack of passengers and this downward spiral persisted until 1963 when the final passenger train along the line was run. Goods services continued for a further fifteen years before the branch closed permanently.

The Leek & Manifold Valley Light Railway

		Date
Passenger service withdrawn	12 March 1934	
Distance	8¾ miles	
Company	Leek & Manifold Valley Light Railway	

Stations closed	Date
Sparrowlee (for Waterfall)	10 March 1964
Beeston Tor	10 March 1934
Grindon	10 March 1934

Stations closed	Date
Thor's Cave (for Wetton)	10 March 1934
Redhurst Crossing Halt	10 March 1934
Wetton Mill	10 March 1934
Butterton	10 March 1934
Ecton (for Warslow)	10 March 1934
Hulme End	10 March 1964

Beeston Tor, 28 June 1933.

Thor's Cave (for Whetton).

The Leek & Manifold Valley Light Railway was authorised by the 1896 Light Railway Act, yet from the moment it opened in June 1904 the line struggled financially despite the (reluctant) backing of the NSR. Even after the 'Knotty' built a standard gauge feeder line from Leek Brook to the L&MVLR at Waterhouses in 1905 losses continued to mount.

Butterton.

The main reason for this was that the L&MVLR was unable to build up a strong freight business to sustain it. To try and salvage the situation the company proposed extending its route through to Buxton but this was blocked by local landowners and the NSR. Likewise, a proposal that the 'Knotty' absorb the light railway got nowhere.

Ecton.

During the First World War the line did enjoy a successful stint as a route for transporting large quantities of milk, but when peace returned the line slipped back into decline. In 1923 it passed into LMS ownership but the new masters had little interest in maintaining such an out-of-the-way, non-standard branch.

Hulme End.

As losses soared, the LMS announced that all passenger services were to be withdrawn in March 1934. The line was then lifted and the route became a footpath.

Locomotive No. 2 at Hulme End with the 3.45 p.m. service to Waterhouses, 29 April 1933.

Leek Brook to Waterhouses

Passenger service withdrawn	28 September 1935
Distance	8½ miles
Company	North Staffordshire Railway

Stations closed	Date
Bradnop	30 September 1935

Stations closed	Date
Chee Dale Halt	30 September 1935
Ipstones	30 September 1935
Winkhill Halt	30 September 1935
Caldon Low Halt	30 September 1935
Waterhouses	30 September 1935

Bradnop, 1905.

This branch was built specifically to act as a feeder line for the L&MVLR. The NSR was less than enthusiastic about it and progress was slow which led to the L&MVLR opening in 1904 before the NSR's link was ready. This forced the 'Knotty' to introduce steam buses to temporarily transfer passengers from Leek Brook to the L&MVLR. This arrangement lasted until July 1905.

The new branch aroused protests from the business community of Leek who believed that providing the people of Waterhouses with a link to Stoke (via Leek Brook Junction and then on to the Biddulph Valley) would affect their livelihoods. Leek was the local market town and the traders there didn't want anybody going elsewhere to buy and sell their own produce.

Locomotive No. 2 at Waterhouses with the 3.45 p.m. service from Hulme End, 29 April 1933.

Waterhouses.

To pacify these complaints the NSR added a spur at Leek Brook Junction to enable direct running of trains between Leek and Waterhouses. This did away with the need for trains to carry out a reversing manoeuvre at Leek Brook and ensured that Leek remained competitive. Limestone traffic from the nearby Caldon Quarry also started using the branch instead of the narrow-gauge tramway to Froghall in the Churnet Valley. The reliance upon freight became increasingly important after the First World War as passenger numbers along the line tailed off. After Grouping there was little the LMS could do to arrest this slide and so it came as little surprise when passenger trains were withdrawn completely during 1935. Goods trains lasted until 1943 when the whole line was closed, bar a section of track from Caldon to Leek Brook Junction. This remained open to enable limestone trains to continue and is still in occasional use today as a freight-only spur.

The Trentham Branch

		Date
Passenger service withdrawn	1 October 1957	
Distance	1/4 miles	
Company	North Staffordshire Railway	
Stations closed		
Trentham Park		1 October 1957
Hanford Road Halt		2 April 1913
Trentham		2 March 1964

Trentham Station.

Approved in August 1907, this short branch was the last of its kind to be built by the NSR. It was intended to provide a connection from Trentham on the main line between Stoke and Stone with the Trentham Gardens recreational centre. This had once been the ancestral home to the Dukes of Sutherland but had been converted into a wildfowl reserve, clay pigeon shooting area and fun fair. The line opened in April 1910 and was soon busy with passenger traffic even though the gardens were within reasonable walking distance of Trentham station itself! The intermediate stop at Hanford Road was not a success and closed during 1913. The line passed into LMS management after 1923 but passenger services along it came to an end in September 1939 as more and more visitors to Trentham Gardens took to using the local bus service or their own motor cars. During the Second World War the branch regained some prominence when the Bank of England's Clearing House temporarily relocated to Trentham Gardens from London for security reasons. However, after 1945 the line saw little use except for the odd excursion and was closed completely in the autumn of 1957.

Closed stations on lines still open to passenger services

Line/service

West Coast Main Line

Stations closed	Date
Colwich	3 February 1958
Great Hayward	6 January 1947
Hixon Halt	6 January 1947
Weston & Ingestre	6 January 1947
Sandon	6 January 1947

Stations closed	Date
Aston-by-Stone	6 January 1947
Trentham Junction	2 March 1964
Sideway Halt	2 April 1923
Mount Pleasant Halt	30 September 1918
Cliffe Vale	31 July 1865
Shelton	2 March 1964
Chatterley	27 September 1948

Colwich Station.